I Am Beautiful

Written by Beautiful Fire:
NOUSHKA

DEDICATION

To:

Our refined, passionate flames within the beautiful realm of

I Am.

Copyright © 2023 I Am Beautiful Fire. All rights reserved. No part of this publication may be reproduced, stored in a retrieval system, stored in a database and/or published in any form or by any means, electronic, mechanical, photocopying, recording or otherwise, without the prior written permission of the publisher.

To request permission contact
collections@iambeautifulfire.com
ISBN: 979-8-9871870-0-5

Get 7 Ways to Live Your Life Ablaze Free!

www.IAmBeautifulFire.com/7ways

This free guide will remind your fiery passions to flow from the inside out.

A note for you *Beautiful*:
Please write a fiery five-star review
for this collection at
www.iambeautifulfire.com/review

FIERY CONTENTS

Acknowledgments   i

Refined

Hello beautiful 3

Flames bellowed "Become" 4
Foundation renewed 5
Beneficial fire 6
Set apart 7
Stellar cast 8
Creator's dough 9
Maestro 10
Reflection's flame 12
Handcuffs off now 13
No bars 14
Fortified 15
Tick! Tick! Boom! 16
Vindicated flames 17
Slumber no more 18
Bulldozer 19
Director's cut 20
Firestorms 21
Oneness tree 22
Came out unscathed 23
Love heals 24
Symphonies of euphony 25
A life of ease 26
No pain to consume 27

Beautiful growth 28
Grafted 29
Fire's glee 30
We are the cocoa 31
Hearts of valor 32
Lights truly attracts 33
Fiery search party 34
Triumphantly we fly 35
Flames' compass 36
Victory dance 37
Valorous queens 38
Purification power of fire 39
All-knowing 40
Music to our own ears 41
I love me first 42
Our fires to waters 43
Came out gold 44
True selves shine 45
Forever smooth 46
Mirror, mirror 47
Oneness flame 48
Good flames 49
Flames alive 50

FIERY CONTENTS
Passioned

The days of light 53
Happy life day to us 54
Divine mama 55
Beautiful blueprints 56
Life giving recipes 57
Bring the offering 58
Earth, wind, fire 59
No naughty in our paradise 60
Disco of love 61
An intimate affair 62
Full flames 63
Senses 64
Secret place finesse 65
Attended to 66
A divine home 67
Emblemed 68
Fiery inn 69
Friends of the flame 70
Worth the time 71
The fiery cared for 72
It's the village for us 73
Silver spoons 74
Fiery overflow 75
Fiery abodes 76
Guest of love 77
Be unwrapped 78
Our love letter 79
In assurance 80
Paintbrush immaculate 81
Passion blazed by 82
Sit your desires 83
We like it hot 84
Capes of fire 85
Useful 86
Illuminate 87
We go beyond infinity 88
Divine's kitchen 89
We smell eternal fuel 90
Red, orange, blue 91
Clink, clink, clink 92
Sincerely the enamored 93

Rise 94
Love life, amazing 95
Etched into eternity 96
Melodious symphonies 97
Play us a song from our radio 98
Ballads of the blaze 99
Blazing truth tunes 100
Sounds of fire 101
Sweet every-things 102
"Firepop" 103
Dance gracefully 104
The audience will know 105
Authenticated by the divine 106
Deliciously displayed 107
Everything zesty 108
Sun-kissed 109
Strong everyday 110
Pollinating flames 111
No price tags on us 112
Fire's ride 113
Pump's galore 114
Our bats swing flames 115
Embrace the full frame 116
Full glow 117
Campfire queens 118
One with fire blazers 119
Mansions 120
Stood tall 121
Fiery surety 122
Our flavor 123
Clay set vessels 124
The muses of the day 125
Inscribed 126
Fire's femininity 127
Model walk 128
Little red dress 129
Dresses of demure 130
Narrow 131
Trailblazers 132
Placed first 133
A letter from fire 134

ACKNOWLEDGMENTS

I would like to acknowledge:

I Am, and who I was created to be eternally within the *Highest* names of all.

My life advisors, Dr. Anthony Rhodman (www.DrAnthonyRhodman.com) and Dr. Beautiful I Am (www.HealTodayWithJai.com). Because of what they've poured into my life, I Am able to walk in the trueness of everything passionate, refined, and on fire!

French instructor, continuity editor of this collection, and sister, Melodies of Joy (@NoellaNzishura). Our work together on this expression of love blazes on towards eternity.

Author and sister, Corine Marie (www.CorineMarie.com), for igniting me to write poetry again.

Voice coach and sister, Joy Ellis (www.JoyLifeTalent.com), for reminding me in all of our sessions, *Who* goes before all of these spoken words.

Talented artist, and illustrator of this collection, Lauren McElrath (@OfficialArtByHarlem), thank you so much for turning my words into beautiful art.

My Mommy, Mimi, for choosing me and I choosing her, and because of that I could choose to write this collection for such a time as this.

My princess for coming to remind me of who *I Am*.

My brother, Free, for all of his support and love.

To my family and all of my friends, I love you! Thank you!

I AM BEAUTIFUL FIRE

Refined

Refined one:
Pages 2 and 52 has a space to record
foundational fires you'd like remember.

REFINED

Title   Page #

HELLO BEAUTIFUL

Your Title Here: _____

After reading each poem, feel free to give it your own beautiful title.

Ring, ring...
When the phone rings, answer.
It's me calling to tell me, I'm beautiful:

No response, return dialed tone.

Ring, ring...
"Hello?", it's me.
I've called to tell myself I'm beautiful:

No response, return dialed tone.

Planted seeds that my fire shone down
To help me grow.
Officially, I've forgotten the days
I didn't answer the call.

Now, fiery seeds of triumph
Grew abloom to shower me with petals of success;
Returns received from the flamed honeysuckles
Perched roundly on my clear, pristine skin.

Ring, ring...
I answered,
"Hello, it's me. I'm beautiful."

FLAMES BELLOWED "BECOME"

Your Title Here: _____

Flames bellowed:
"BECOME."
I answered with a flicker
And met a full blaze.
A meeting not in vain;
I'm glad I came
Because *flame* showed me
The answers I desired
Dwelled within.
Learned inwardly of the good of myself,
And gloriously accepted accountability
For who I am and who I'll always be:
A divine creator,
So strong,
So bold,
So fiery.
Blessed to have answered the call.

FOUNDATION RENEWED

Your Title Here: _____

Diary,

What a beautiful day!
Today was crowning day;
A homecoming of sorts.
It was fiery,
And I narrate it as such:

What a beautiful day
To quell insecurities
That silence my pops;
Flames came and took all harsh plagues away.
Burned up what did not serve me.
I visited reservoirs where
Fuel tanks stay filled to the brim—
With overflow.
I win;
Always crowned victoriously.
My acceptance speech matches my actions—
I'm filled.
What a beautiful day!

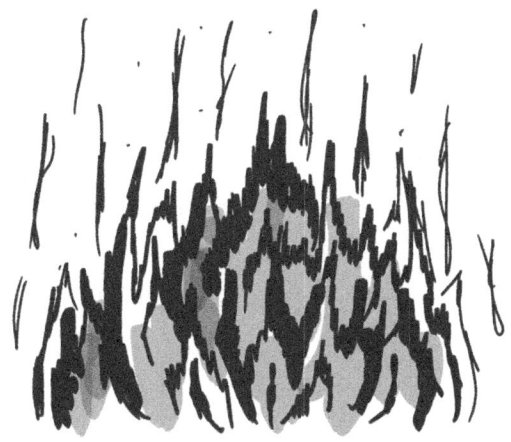

BENEFICIAL FIRE

Your Title Here: _____

For those who want to take an extinguisher
To my flames, this is my response:

I'm no opposition to your true self:
I'm all light—
All necessary.

What they perceive as rage are pleasant flames
Beckoned by refinement's sake—
All necessary.

My fire wraps around the coldest of hearts:
Melting all frigidness,
Purifying all in sight, and
Leaving warmth behind.
I am divine—
Surely necessary.

SET APART

Your Title Here: _____

What others wanted me to cherish as landmarks,
I viewed as prisons that wanted to hold me in—
Put me in a box.

Where limits dwelled,
I eternally quelled.

Statues that commemorated
What they saw fit for me were
Burned up.

Flames cannot be contained
In small spaces with key and lock.

I desire not to conform:
For I was born to stand out.

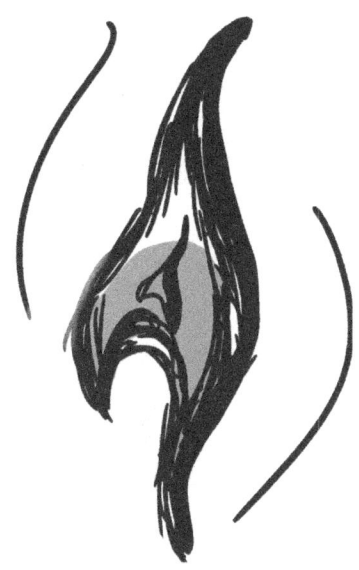

STELLAR CAST

Your Title Here: _____

Limps,
Fright,
Defeat—
Exit stage left.
Limbs made straight,
Now stellar cast.
Curtain calls...
Applauses.
My recitals of *Self*-love lead to
Uproars of
"Encore,
Encore,
Encore."

CREATOR'S DOUGH

Your Title Here: _____

Molded,
Fermented, and
Roasted in the fire:
It's time for my
Divine *Self* to
Arise.

MAESTRO
Your Title Here: _____

Maestro conduct for me a song
With melodic abilities,
Clef notes' rapid fire agilities.
Let's go
To view up close
The waves of the Maestro
That tell me when to
Sing high and
Sing low—
Just right.
Go, go!
I go...
To listen close
To the songs of the Maestro;
Composed to
Refine
Purify
Notes played on high.
Truly this is orchestra defined;
I gather around the Maestro's baton
To hear my flames play on
With melodic abilities,
Clef notes' rapid fire agilities.
I go!
All at once and stay...
To listen, feel, taste, touch, to know
The songs of the Maestro
Composed to
Refine
Purify—
Notes played on high.

REFLECTION'S FLAME
Your Title Here: _____

They said:
"Mademoiselles, put the fire out.
Little ones don't frolic with flames;
They play with toys."

Thought my fire would turn into vengeful rage,
But instead, became
Reflection's flame.

Paid meticulous attention to the
Art of my affection,
Wrote this on the tablets of my heart:
"I am jovial fire:
Entertainment
For days."

HANDCUFFS OFF NOW
Your Title Here: _____

My flames called out:
*"Handcuffs off now.
REVOLT."*

NO BARS

Your Title Here: _____

All hail to the fire that
Burned down prison wards:
No bars.

Innocent.
Thankful
I've been set free.

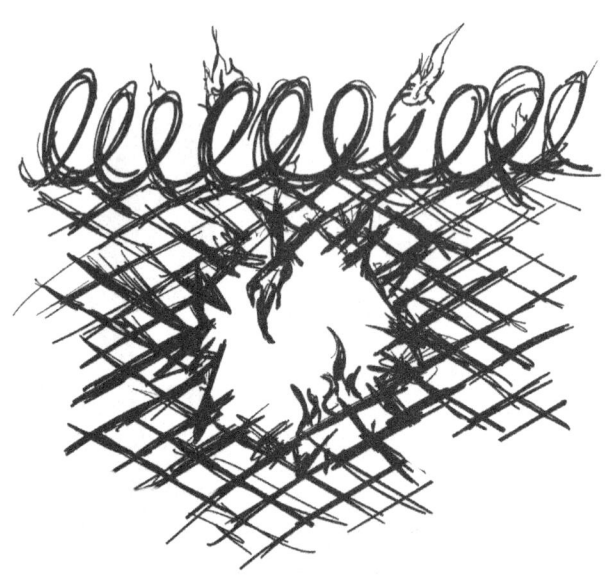

FORTIFIED

Your Title Here: _____

How can someone break my hearts,
If I'm unbreakable?

How can something destroy me,
If fuel abounds internally?

How can anything outside of me stop my fire?

If fire reigns down from inward skies on high,

How can...?

TICK! TICK! BOOM!
Your Title Here: _____

Tick,
Tick,
Boom!
No need to read me my rights.
When the fuse was lit,
I was there.
Everything lost in the explosion was never necessary.

Confession:
"I was an accessory to the affair."

VINDICATED FLAMES

Your Title Here: _____

They came to check the scene:
Scoured it.
At the end, they
Became witnesses to why I'm named,
"Vindicated Flames".

SLUMBER NO MORE

Your Title Here: _____

Wake up!
Arise.
Slumber on my flames
No more.

BULLDOZER

Your Title Here: _____

Barrier: Darkness.

Enters Bulldozer.
Destroys inferiority.

My life is now
Meticulously and
Passionately,
Refined.

DIRECTOR'S CUT
Your Title Here: _____

Lights, Camera, Action!
Don't cut the scenes:
Walk through the fire.
Hold the cuts:
Don't splice it.
I want to see it,
I want to hear it.
I have time:
I'll stay for the *Director's* cut.

FIRESTORMS

Your Title Here: _____

Thankful when fire rains
On dim lit days.
When thunder roars,
I support
My *firestorms.*

ONENESS TREE
Your Title Here: _____

Burn down the forest
Where trees lie with lies that
Yield fruits of death, not life.
Strike the match and watch
Acres of iniquity
Succumb to unified flames:
Sparked to justify and
Purify
All which was never meant to dwell.
Family tree of oneness,
I receive you and cheer
For the burning uproot;
I welcome
All truthful fruit.

CAME OUT UNSCATHED

Your Title Here: _____

No crops harmed:
Forever untouched.
Our portion of protection
Yielded bliss into my fruit—
Refinement was the portion.
I grew:
Weeds scorched,
Seeds remained intact,
Abundance received.
I came out of the fire
Unscathed.

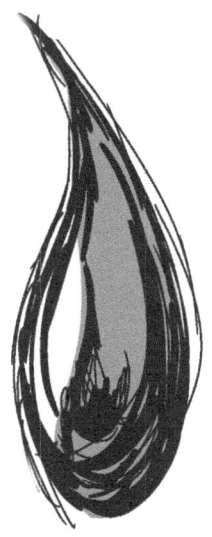

LOVE HEALS

Your Title Here: _____

"Love hurts":
A scorched mantra.
Hymns that yielded no fruit were
Scorched for
Love I've known forever:
Intact with
Patience, and
Kindness,
Truth's essence and resilience
Cleared way for
Repetitions of,
"Love heals."

SYMPHONIES OF EUPHONY

Your Title Here: _____

Sound the horn of blazing triumph:
I've won the wars of old.
My new life of victory,
Received.
The wars that once raged within are
No more.
Now I know...
To live in pure streams of harmony,
I must connect to *flow.*
Symphonies of euphony
Stream
From high places,
From *ONE's* spaces,
So all can see and live in blissful accord
Within,
With thee.

A LIFE OF EASE

Your Title Here: _____

For me who burned pillowcases
With streams of disdain,
I cry no more.
I unveiled who I was created to be as
I wiped off the toxic flows of tears
That kept me in darkness.
My new life of bliss called out:
"No need for tears—
You know who you are,
From within,
Streams of *life.*"
Eternally,
A life of ease.

NO PAIN TO CONSUME

Your Title Here: _____

Waiter: "How would you like that prepared?"

Me: "Ashes, Brimstone, and Sulfur!"

Waiter: "Everything good?"

Us: "Yes, tell chef, thank you. She helped me escape the taste of death. No pain to consume. Check, please."

BEAUTIFUL GROWTH
Your Title Here: _____

Discarded from the cremation were
The remains from the pain:
Never of gain.
What they told me would hurt was my seed under soil,
Waiting to come up.
Ashes for beauty—
Such beautiful growth.

GRAFTED

Your Title Here: _____

1st degree,
2nd degree,
3rd degree, and
4th degree
Burns:
Be gone.
My flames cannot be described with numbers.
I've blazed
Away from all that attempted to measure me
With lies to contrive the
Evidence of damages I've abandoned.
My blaze caused no harm
Because what was scorched
Was never meant to be.
I am *grafted*, and
Always
Renewed.

FIRE'S GLEE

Your Title Here: _____

Fire's wrath,
Destroyed.
Fire's glee,
Restored.

WE ARE THE COCOA

Your Title Here: _____

On red and pink day,
I used to yearn for their affection.
Now from within,
Self-love warms my heart.
Pulled up a log, and
Sat in front of the flames.
I brought no chocolate to the bonfire
Yet memorabilia of old
To watch the prehistoric go.
I'm now alive—
Divine.
I am sweet:
I am the cocoa.

HEARTS OF VALOR

Your Title Here: _____

Adorned with hearts of valor,
I'm not wounded: simply refined
By fire's flame.
I won the battle
Between old and new:
Truth defends me.
The fight
Was not my own, for I was
More than conquerors all along.
I stand in what I know,
Who I am,
Where I'm from,
Why I'm here,
Where I'm going,
And all that I can do.

LIGHT TRULY ATTRACTS

Your Title Here: _____

"Dimness stay back":
Brought our fuel to your lack;
Knew it was possible to flame forward:
My light truly attracts.

FIERY SEARCH PARTY
Your Title Here: _____

With ignited torches,
I made way out of caves.
Left dimness to flee towards fire,
In anticipation of all that I could be.
Decapitated all pains, and
Cleared the way
For my very own search party—
A fiery blaze.

TRIUMPHANTLY WE FLY

Your Title Here: _____

Burned through the cocoon that
My blaze could hold no more.
Ready to journey through the course;
Triumphantly,
I fly.

FLAMES' COMPASS

Your Title Here: _____

I made it out of the
Woods;
The flames showed me
Which way to go.

VICTORY DANCE

Your Title Here: _____

Awakened by the crackling pops of
The fire I set last night:
Victory dance to the fire,
Victory dance to the pops—
A melodious rhythm,
A sound for all to hear.
All rebels to my goodness incinerated by the
Fire that blazed through the night.
Leaving a canister empty and nothing
But refinement behind;
A refinement so pure,
Shining brighter than the highest carats of gold.
It was the purity for me:
My gold within that shined on out
As I danced to my reflection—
Intimately, lovingly, and passionately.
It was the fire for me:
Victory dance to the fire,
Victory dance to the pops.

VALOROUS QUEENS

Your Title Here: _____

Victory, victory, victory:
These are the roars of
Triumphant sounds.
Because I am a fiery valorous *queen*
Courageous in face of adversity.

PURIFICATION POWER OF FIRE

Your Title Here: _____

My fire appeared and
Left complexions of perfection.
A purified mirror always
Glows, glows, glows:
> Excellence personified.
> Purification power of fire is here,
> No blemish appears—
> Pristine reflections.

ALL - KNOWING

Your Title Here: _____

When I looked at myself,
All parts of me,
I saw where fire raged and
Where dimness lurked.
For every divine question answered,
Fuel abound.
For every query neglected,
Flickers prolonged.
"Leave dimness alone," said my divine within.
So I received my fuel for the flicker because
I was full blaze all along.

MUSIC TO OUR OWN EARS

Your Title Here: _____

Music lives within,
So I burned records
Where disdain used to play.
I remember the days when
I engulfed all noise—
Uproars that kept fingers to ears.
I no longer have to clog
My lobes:
Now free
To hear and
Receive
Precious revelation,
Track after track—
No skips.

I LOVE ME FIRST

Your Title Here: _____

The day we met,
There were *dialogues* consumed by full fiery flame:
"I've never loved anybody as much as I love you,"
I couldn't say—
It wasn't true.
So, these are the words that I spoke:
"I loved me first;
Therefore,
I can love you."

OUR FIRES TO WATERS

Your Title Here: _____

Not afraid when water hoses come.
I light the way for them to travel through the dark.
Lighters of the night, and
Lighters of the day:
I correlate our use with theirs.

This is our fate:
Working together
To take our fire to waters—
Atlantic.
There is truly nothing to fear.
Everything helps my blaze.

CAME OUT GOLD
Your Title Here: _____

Threw the urn away—
No old.
Not an ash behind:
Came out gold.

TRUE SELVES SHINE

Your Title Here: _____

I burned to the depths
All superficial coverings,
Leaving myself bare and warm
At the same time.
I'm naked from destruction,
Adorned by flames of creation, and
Filled with divinity—
My true self shines.

FOREVER SMOOTH

Your Title Here: _____

I came out on the other side purified:
Gold shown through, and
Every imperfection removed.
All groves of disdain incinerated:
I am smooth,
Pure, and
Polished.
Dwellings of love,
Light, and
Everything divine:
I came out on the other side,
Even,
No dents—
The forever smooth.

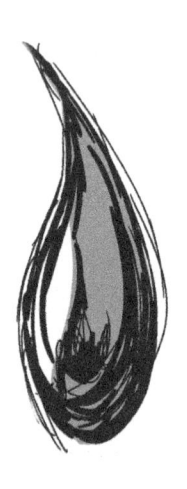

MIRROR, MIRROR

Your Title Here: _____

Flawless complexions, and
Reflections of perfection:
Purified mirrors are
Pristine.
Power of our fire,
Blemish free.
Inwardly, I bellowed:
*"Once tarnished perception,
Return no more."*
My inward mirror spoke back,
*"You are the divinity of them all,
Keep going,
Keep going,
Don't look back."*

ONENESS FLAME

Your Title Here: _____

Once and for all,
Adorned with grins of perfection.
What was beneath crooked smiles is now
Inflamed by love's true passion.
Everything burned was not in vain because it
Brought me to beams of
Oneness flame.

GOOD FLAMES

Your Title Here: _____

I've grown:
Expanded into full manifestation of my flames.
Completely dismissed
External innuendos that suggest
My blaze isn't good enough.
Boasting in tiny seeds, my
Flames sprout high,
Forevermore.
I am authenticated by the *One* up high,
Who's up close to me.
Where I spark,
I arise.

FLAMES ALIVE

Your Title Here: _____

Combusted:
Burned to a crisp all deceit that spoke
Against who I am...
With lies farthest from truth.
I stretched my flame far and wide
To destroy all lies that dwelled in darkness.
Word came back that they're no more;
No evidence left.
No doom for me—
I am alive.

I AM BEAUTIFUL FIRE

Passioned

Passionate one:
On the next page, there's space to record
foundational fires you'd like remember.

PASSIONED

Title   Page #

THE DAYS OF LIGHT

Your Title Here: _____

This is a praise for my process from
Flicker to flame:

Infilled with passionate love,
I know who I am, and
Why I came.
I am free to forgive, forget, and blaze on.
I cover and honor my days completely:
My past in praise,
My present in gratitude, and
My future in thanksgiving.

I am new,
The days of light.

HAPPY LIFE DAY TO US

Your Title Here: _____

Fires blaze as streamers
Hang upon the wall:
It's a party in honor of me.
I gather around
The cake to receive...
I would never blow out
My own fate.
With eternity's secure,
I sashay through the room
And sing to my tune:
"Happy Life Day to Me!"

DIVINE MAMA

Your Title Here: _____

I've grown so much:
From a child afraid of flickers
To a bold beauty who
Embrace full flames.
Divine Mama,
Look at me...
I'm proud of me.

BEAUTIFUL BLUEPRINTS

Your Title Here: _____

Beautiful blueprints are
Penned by *mighty* hands.
Never led by chance but
Always intentional.
Bonded with *One's* vision;
Side by side with those who meticulously,
And strategically,
Plan.

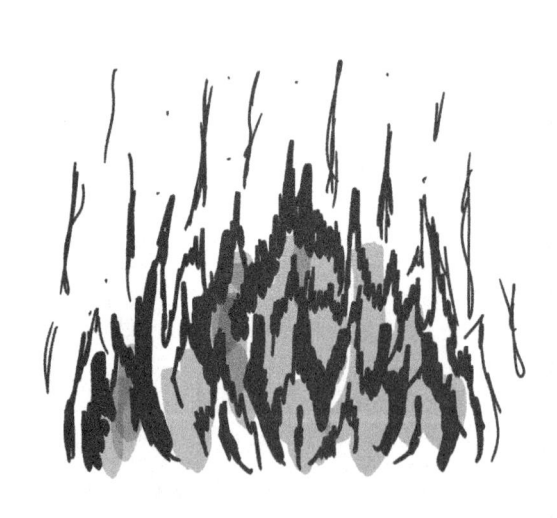

LIFE-GIVING RECIPES

Your Title Here: _____

At the depths of my core lies a fire that brews
The life-giving recipes of simplicity.
There's an overflowing cauldron
In which I came to portion:
No witch,
Nor broom,
Just firm lucidity.
When fires brew, who knew
That the recipes would be so good!
Simplistically divine,
I am recipes defined
With serving sides just right.
My creation
Quelled all plights
Of those who hungered within our sight.
I ate first, and
Portioned last.

BRING THE OFFERING

Your Title Here: _____

Here is my offering of
Fuel, fan, and wood:
Guaranteed to keep you lit all night.
Flames
Defined by the Divine,
Dance just right.
This is *Love:*
Pleasure personified.
I honor myself for the fuel,
The fan, and
The wood
That lives within.

EARTH, WIND, FIRE

Your Title Here: _____

Earth encompasses, and
Wind compliments;
Fire receives all.
Nothing is a threat to me, for
All elements are of
Great benefit to me.

NO NAUGHTY IN OUR PARADISE

Your Title Here: _____

I lit the *coals*,
Made a feast,
Sat,
Dined, and
Served *Passion's* piece:
First to myself,
Then to others.
No naughty in my paradise—
Just flames,
All night.

DISCO OF LOVE

Your Title Here: _____

Dirty dancing?
No.
Soot?
None on the dance floor.
Sways of romance
Have come to dance
With me:
Flame's sashays and
Passionate tangos.
Pure twirls within
For I?
Why...
Yes!

AN INTIMATE AFFAIR

Your Title Here: _____

Never would I,
Nor do I,
Sell myself short;
I do not let others *in* without an *RSVP*.

FULL FLAMES

Your Title Here: _____

Welcome to *Theater Ablaze,*
Where passionate visions thrive and
Powerless flickering's turn into
Full flames.
Indeed,
I've arrived to my own showing;
On the big screen are
All fiery films.

SENSES

Your Title Here: _____

Opened eyes,
See for me.
Unclogged lobes,
Hear for me.
Adorned tongues,
Taste for me.
Nostrils' strength,
Smell for me.
Fiery hands,
Feel for me.

SECRET PLACE FINESSE

Your Title Here: _____

They ask me what makes my fire go boom:

It's the quiet time in my
Grand still room.
Private rooms where
Love pours in as
I sit with self in eternity;
There's no end
Nor beginning.

Secret place finessed:
All blessed.

ATTENDED TO

Your Title Here: _____

"Love on pump one please."
Gorgeous sights to see, and
Fueling stations
For all—
For me.

I sit within;
They fuel throughout.

Eternal love received;
Attended to as
I... cleave.

I knew my blaze could not go without
The propellant force of Oneness that
Eternally flows throughout.

A DIVINE HOME
Your Title Here: _____

A divine home is
Filled with passionate motifs and
Unbreakable
Refined artifacts.
My bed welcomes O*neness,* day and dusk;
Couches sit my company ever so presently.
My home: a dwelling of divinity.
Foyers of tranquility
Made this house a home.
Dedicated all within and
Throughout with
Tele-a-visions that play my divine destinies—
Beset by serenity.

EMBLEMED

Your Title Here: _____

Luxuriously
Emblemed:
The Fiery,
I Am.

FIERY INN

Your Title Here: _____

I'm all in;
This is where I reside—
At the *Fiery Inn.*

FRIENDS OF THE FLAME

Your Title Here: _____

Comrades of the blaze,
I hang with what burns.
Outsiders thought I'd gone astray,
Led by the wrong crowd—
False.
I commune with what crackles;
There's no shame in my game—
My flames are good.
They see them,
They see me;
Just the way I want it.
Dance high for me!
Tear down for me!
Flames are good company:

Best friends,
For life.

WORTH THE TIME

Your Title Here: _____

Abundantly good company
Is worth the time,
And all things more.
I adore every moment with you:
From lifetimes,
Ages, to
Eternal galore.

THE FIERY CARED FOR

Your Title Here: _____

Wrapped in the serenity of all passion,
I am looked after as
Newborn,
Child, and
Elder.

My newness
Adorned,
My playfulness
Cherished, and
My wisdom
Respected.

I am
Sincerely and
Passionately,
The Fiery Cared For.

IT'S THE VILLAGE FOR US

Your Title Here: _____

With a whole village
Behind me, inside me, and around me...
I thrive, smile, and shine.
I always knew that the village lived within:
My inward village raised me—
Refined me.
The village spoke well of me;
They taught me to speak well of myself,
And others.
If you come a little closer,
You'll also see that
This isn't just me:
It's the village.

SILVER SPOONS

Your Title Here: _____

A true confidant
Showed up, and
Removed all tarnishes from
The silver spoons,
I was always meant to have.
She...
Revealed what fed me...
Oh my...
Such fiery cutlery!

FIERY OVERFLOW

Your Title Here: _____

Cups of fiery overflow are
Never empty:
Always full!

FIERY ABODES

Your Title Here: _____

I don't have to wail anymore nor
Feel inferior,
As if I'm not adorned.
Fire came and lit my life:
I don't
Cry anymore,
Fight anymore, nor
Lie anymore.
Thankful for *fire* that called me out of basements,
Into fiery abodes.

GUEST OF LOVE

Your Title Here: _____

Housewarming guest,
Welcome to my abode
Where gifts are present in
Our presence.
I've unwrapped for me and
For you,
Bows of red and
Blue.
Guest of love,
I've warmed this place with me in mind
And you.

BE UNWRAPPED

Your Title Here: _____

My note to a friend:

Fiery one,
Within coal brimmed spaces,
Bring your presents—
All your presence.
Entwined within flame's wrappings,
You are a gift.
With a bow,
Be unwrapped.

OUR LOVE LETTER

Your Title Here: _____

My love letter to the *welder:*

Thank you for bonding my inward parts as one.
In your love,
There is no pain,
Nor crying in the rain.
I'm bonded by the greatest
Love of all.

IN ASSURANCE

Your Title Here: _____

Where else can I go?
There is no question of *Passion's* love for me.
You are *Great Fire:*
The first *Giver,*
Provider, and
Sustainer.
Certainly,
I am in assurance.

PAINTBRUSH IMMACULATE

Your Title Here: _____

To my Divine Artist:

Paintbrush immaculate,
No one paints flames like you.
The stroke of your brush is the
Precision I always desired.
My muse, I muse:
For, the cruise of your brush has been oh so smooth.
As I gaze at skies you meticulously designed,
I'm left amused by you.
Artiste, you are an artisan with a good eye;
You saw me before time.
From eternal waves of your brush,
I came alive—
Arose from the
Divine canvases of
Passion's artistic design.

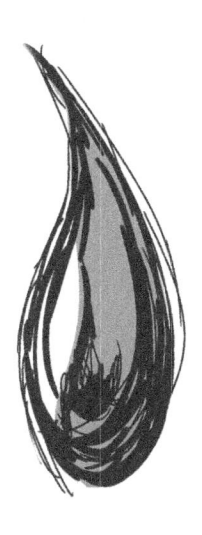

PASSION BLAZED BY

Your Title Here: _____

Divine natural hues,
Color towns with tones of fervor.
As the flames stop by,
They all know
Passion blazed by and
Nothing would be the same.
For the warmth on the faces of those they love
Were engulfed in hues of
Ruby,
Amber, and
Sapphire.
From wells filled with *eternal*,
This romance would become *life's* standard.
For I am…
Well-intended…
Fiery flames.

SIT YOUR DESIRES

Your Title Here: _____

Come close by
On warm summer nights
To gaze at the colors of
Reds intertwined.
May you catch wind that my benches
Sit your desires.

Love,
The *fire*.

WE LIKE IT HOT

Your Title Here: _____

No cold!
I am the strike needed to light all coals.
I thank myself for showing up—
I like it hot.

CAPES OF FIRE

Your Title Here: _____

Save the day, why don't you?
Goblins of dimness don't stand a chance around you.

Supernatural in every way;
Adorned with capes of fire.

The heroic acts of your blaze are a sight for all to see.
Arsenal equipped with the fuel of love to light the way.

Fear cowers at the mere flicker of your power:
Miraculous.

Light the night, why don't you?
Go ahead, and light the day.

USEFUL

Your Title Here: _____

They raise me at concerts, and
Light me for intimate dinners.
My existence is of practicality,
Intimacy, and
Dependability—
I am *useful*.

ILLUMINATE

Your Title Here: _____

I illuminated the faces of those whose
Prisons no longer served them.
My flames snuffed
Where contempt once grew.
I cleared out all dim spaces as
I turned them into abodes filled with radiance:
Gave them permission to live in full display.
I thank the divine for time, and
Grace to do what I was
Born to do—
Illuminate.

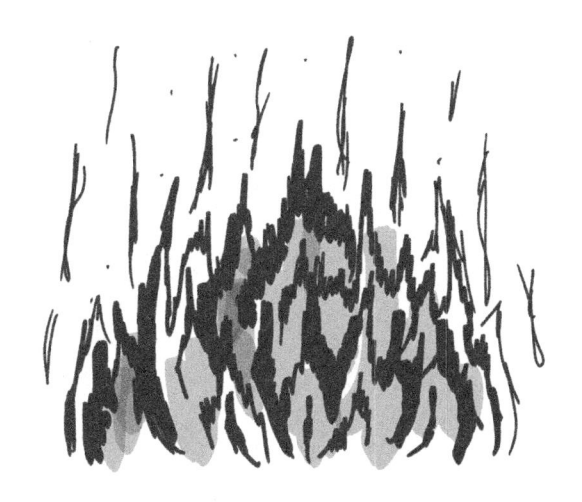

Your Title Here: _____

More than rubies,
More than gold:
I'm incomparable to material.
I myself thaw
All hearts of complacency.
Far superior to pearls,
I control entire worlds;
Also, the earth is at my feet.
This passion is never weak,
Fading,
Nor ending.
I go beyond infinity;
No stone to solidify my yes.

Engaged, and
Betrothed:
Made one with all possibilities.

DIVINE'S KITCHEN

Your Title Here: _____

In my kitchen, they can stand the heat:
This fire ain't for the weak.
They came for proof, but
I scorched everything bleak
That imprisoned their glorious spreads.
It was necessary for me to inspire them to
Ignite their own stoves, so they could
Prepare meals that fed
Their souls first, then others.
They came to the kitchen, and
I asked if they could stand the heat;
Their head nods sufficed— though bleak.
I burned all which wouldn't help the
Nourishment of their souls, and mines—
Leaving not a crisp behind.
I was kind because my fire isn't mean,
But intentionally divine.

WE SMELL ETERNAL FUEL

Your Title Here: _____

Do I smell that?
Why yes...
The sweet fumes of eternal fuel.
All of my senses are heightened by passion;
Today, I marvel at the scent.
Yes, I smell the expectation of burning love
From a mile away.
As with all things,
I know if it smells good, it must...
The sweet aroma of what was cooked by my fuel,
Keep ovens lit all night.
Why yes...
I smell that...
Eternal fuel.

RED, ORANGE, BLUE

Your Title Here: _____

So this is love?
Fire burning
Oh so
Brightly,
Vividly, and
Passionately.
Open wide beautiful;
Show us your transparency:
Hues of
Red,
Orange, and
Blue.
I want to see you,
Hear you, and
Feel you.
I want you...
All of you.

CLINK, CLINK, CLINK

Your Title Here: _____

May I propose a toast from
Our trailblazing creator that lives within...
I'm never parched for the
Love within has
No end.
I raise my glass, for I
Agree that from within is where
My refreshment lies:
Eternal droughts destroyed,
Forevermore.

SINCERELY THE ENAMORED

Your Title Here: _____

Peace wrote a letter...

It left my
Flames signed,
Sealed, and
Enamored.

RISE

Your Title Here: _____

Dear all who want to fall for me:

Fall for me?
No...
I've never seen flames cower for another.
I want you to stand tall for me:
Be bold for me.
Passionate lovers always rise above.
I want you to stand on your own two feet:
Not dim out, nor be weak.
You'll never have to fall for me.
We'll each rise to the occasion;
Never validated by persuasion,
But liberation.
So...
Stand tall for me—
Be bold for me.

LOVE LIFE, AMAZING

Your Title Here: _____

How's my love life?
Love life amazing,
Steady blazing,
Never failing,
Ending, nor
Fading.

Signs of fire,
Let me show you that
Love soars,
Forevermore.
When they ask me,
I answer swiftly

From banners of amóre:
"Love life, amazing,
Steady blazing, ..."

ETCHED INTO ETERNITY

Your Title Here: _____

My name is in high places—
Power-fueled spaces.
Inscribed in truth,
Italicized by the divine,
<u>Underlined</u>,
UPPERCASED...
I'm the fiery **bold**.
I don't just cheer when dimness flees,
But also at thoughts that my name is written
In the books of life.
I am engraved by fire;
I am etched into eternity.

MELODIOUS SYMPHONIES
Your Title Here: _____

My mind strung in divinity,
Melt cold hearts,
String by string.

My harps strum in light,
Make soft compositions,
Line by line.

My songs reset others
To hear their own
Divinely-stringed
Orchestras.

I am fires,
Melodious symphonies, with
Resonators crafted by the
Most High Living Luthier.

PLAY US A SONG FROM OUR RADIO

Your Title Here: _____

Play me a song from my radio:
A song of victory,
With fiery beats of triumphant abilities.

On my way,
I'll play
Songs of love, light, and everything nice...
With blazes for treble
And all refinement in sight.

Sights just right;
No plights,
On our way.

Play me a song from my radio:
A tune of refinery,
After repeated agility of
Fueled-laced trajectories
Towards *gold* victories.

Play me a song from my radio:
My radio of solidarity,
Where I'm one with disc jockeys
That don't mind playing repeats
Of those who live beautifully,
Victory after victory.

Play me a song from my radio:
I'm on the way.
I'll let it play—
Respectfully.

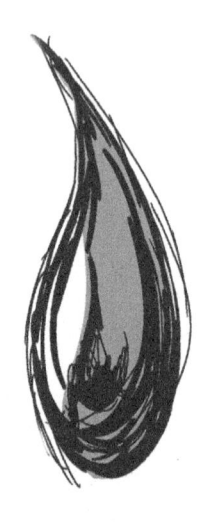

BALLADS OF THE BLAZE

Your Title Here: _____

When the ballad begins,
They know I compose from within.

I perform my...
Songs of sentiments,
Ballads of roses,
Bouquets, and
Enchants:
This is an eternal song.

From me,
Ballads of the blaze.

BLAZING TRUTH TUNES

Your Title Here: _____

The music I love the most
Is that which I make:
Rhythm and
True love's melodies.
I am creator of my reality.
I don't let outside radios
Tell me what to sing;
I belt what I know.
I love beautiful kinds of music—
Particularly, my own.

SOUNDS OF FIRE

Your Title Here: _____

Sounds of my fire
Create,
Vibrate, and
Transmit.

SWEET EVERY-THINGS

Your Title Here: _____

I say no to murmurs of sweet nothing's.

My inward lobes welcome
Whispers from who we are...
Completely adorned:
"I'm all I've ever wanted
And more":

Sweet flamed *every-things.*

"FIREPOP"

Your Title Here: _____

Bitter taste?
No.
Flames are
Sweet as candy—
Firepop.

DANCE GRACEFULLY

Your Title Here: _____

Flames of glory,
Dance gracefully.
The fluidity of our sway
Is a wonderful sight to see—
What a glorious display!

THE AUDIENCE WILL KNOW

Your Title Here: _____

Take the stage and the audience will know
That this all happened before the lights arose.
From internal performances,
This show comes from the strong:
I perform well, for I know the
Light
And *Truth*.
Now all know that
They can live to display
Their fiery passions too.

AUTHENTICATED BY THE DIVINE

Your Title Here: _____

My warm performance is
Never cowardly,
But fiery.

Authenticated by the divine—
My light is a byproduct of my
Beautiful burning stage.

I'm never late:
I do everything from love.
Besides...
What others feel is simply
A byproduct
Of my fiery burning blaze.

DELICIOUSLY DISPLAYED

Your Title Here: _____

The icing on the cake is
My journey:
Deliciously displayed and
Fierily baked.

EVERYTHING ZESTY

Your Title Here: _____

My blaze stirs love's marmalade to a boil.
With great enthusiasm,
I bring the sweet zest of life for
All to taste, and spread:
Knives already set out.
With great zeal,
I prepare the preserve.
My recipes never fail
To make everything tasty,
Everything zesty.

SUN-KISSED

Your Title Here: _____

My beautiful fireball is
Tantalized,
Sun-kissed, and
All fiery—
All bliss.

STRONG EVERYDAY

Your Title Here: _____

I am bold and brazen;
I am courageous flames—
Strong everyday.

POLLINATING FLAMES

Your Title Here: _____

Butterfly wings...
Immaculate.
Bee stripes...
Purpose *full*.
Pollinating flames...
All fly high.

NO PRICE TAGS ON US

Your Title Here: _____

Low ego,
You won't find any price tags on me.
I am are priceless—
Perfectly fashioned with
No replica in sight.
The fiery eternal made me;
I'm not for sale
Nor on clearance, and
Never half off.

No price tags on me!

FIRE'S RIDE

Your Title Here: _____

Fire's ride cost more
For those unwilling to pay—
My attraction is
An inward blaze.
Higher places forfeit the fake
For all spirited truth.
Coasters of love
Soar towards oneness' climbs.
My question is...
Can they roll this coast?

PUMP'S GALORE

Your Title Here: _____

Love's ride
Blazes from within,
Where the *Divine* sparks vehicles towards destinies—
Where ember roam freely.
I'm filled up
From those that never run out of fuel.
Fueled passionately
From high places, these
Journeys, I'm
Equipped for.
I travel ever so rapidly for
I was born to travel diligently.
I glean from places of ignition
Towards destinies so heavenly.

OUR BAT'S SWING FLAMES

Your Title Here: _____

My bat swing flames on the fields of life where
Lies any form of tournament.
I never lose:
All parts of me
Always win.
With *my referee* in sight,
Darkness never stands a chance.
When *I* show up,
I hit home runs.

Victoriously,
The Fire

EMBRACE THE FULL FRAME
Your Title Here: _____

I've worked through the times when the flash
Intimidated me;
Embraced the full frame of my flames.
Took a picture
To recite a thousand words
That quelled all disdain.
These are passionate love gains
For me and those around.
My expressed passion,
Love, and
Light
Are the cause of my
Physique wrapped in amóre.
Now...
Show me my photograph...
Ahhh
I'm gorgeous—
Inflamed.

FULL GLOW

Your Title Here: _____

Want to serenade me with what I already know?
So be it—
Let it be so.
As a reminder,
I'm not in need of anything.
I already know
Who I am, and
What I want—
Full glow.
I know I gleam the brightest;
They come alongside me
To show that they glow
Their own way,
All rightfully so.
I'm thankful they know
Both my fire and theirs.
Orchestrated a parade in honor of us
Blowing past needing to be affirmed from those without.

Warmest Regards,
The Fiery

Your Title Here: _____

The days when I craved
The sweet touch of those outside
Cease to amaze.
Amazingly,
I now see,
Stunned by my own electricity;
I've arrived,
Alive...
To my own capabilities.
Inward bonfires arise!
I, the *Campfire Queen,*
Have come to eat
Where loving s'mores are infinite.
My love is what we needed all along:
My touch,
Light, and
Fire.

ONE WITH FIRE BLAZERS

Your Title Here: _____

With hoses filled...
Pacific...
Firefighters were sent
To put out my flames.
When they arrived on the scene,
I convincingly
Turned them into fire-blazers;
Showing them where to direct their affections—
All fittingly so.
Long ago,
They committed truancy
Against their true passions—
Not rightfully so.
Now,
We blaze as one!

MANSIONS

Your Title Here: _____

In the old tiny home,
Inferiority laid its head.
I arose:
I slumber no more and
Rest in mansions now.

STOOD TALL

Your Title Here: _____

Stood tall...
As the flames within
Burned high with
No end.
Now towering
As *real* flames do.

FIERY SURETY

Your Title Here: _____

I am surety—
No ambiguity,
But fluidity.
Blazing through
Everything adulterated,
I am pure...
Pure in who I am.
I am secure...
Secure in who I am.
I am confident in my abilities;
My coverage stretches far to lands of purity—
Certainly demure.

OUR FLAVOR

Your Title Here: _____

What flavor do I like?
Love?
Light?
Fiery ice?

Hmmm...

I like...

Warmth to the touch.
Everything good at once.

CLAY-SET VESSELS

Your Title Here: _____

The *Potter* molds
Blazin'
Clay-set
Vessels...

I am one.

THE MUSE OF THE DAY

Your Title Here: _____

I hold hands with fire
Every day as I acquire
Love grasps with victories of
Agape.
I high-five with fire,
Inspiring all to aspire as they become
Muse's flame.
Others do inquire,
So I write them letters to ignite flames from within:

I sign
With Love,
The Muse of the Day.

INSCRIBED

Your Title Here: _____

I rewrote Scarlet's letter
For notes where truth resides:
No lies.
Written in permanent ink,
There's no shame
Nor guilt
Inscribed by the *One*.
From the beginnings of time,
Always chosen, and
Heading towards visions set.

I am *One* with the plan, and
One with the Divine.

FIRE'S FEMININITY

Your Title Here: _____

I am wonderful,
Elegant, and
Full of strength.
Embodiment of the tenderly is my
Feminine fire sashaying
Through *wonder's* night.
I check my sight to make sure
It aligns with the *Visionaries,*
Then I proceed forth.

MODEL WALK

Your Title Here: _____

The torch within lights
The runway:
I stand tall,
I strut,
I blaze the way—
Model walk.

LITTLE RED DRESS

Your Title Here: _____

Little red dress:

I put you on to gather around
Fire's romantic blaze.
With ruby gowns,
I turn flicks into
Full flames of appeal;
With a planned ensemble,
I turn soot
Into devoted flames.
This is an attire fit for
Who I am, and
Why I came.

DRESSES OF DEMURE

Your Title Here: _____

I receive
Fathers, mothers,
Brothers and sisters...
That spin ball gowns of fire.
When the clock strikes twelve,
My pumpkin doesn't rot—
Flames still blaze.
I don't need,
But allow a prince
To enhance *the* kingdom
Within and without—
It's ours.

NARROW

Your Title Here: _____

My true essence
Aligns.
My fire burns straight
On roads of harmony:
I blaze on well.

TRAILBLAZERS

Your Title Here: _____

My flames left
Tire-marked gravel
Due to *Love's*
Trailblazing
Ride.
I've journeyed well,
I journey well,
And we will continue to...

PLACED FIRST

Your Title Here: _____

Fire won me the gold—
Perfect scores.
Here's
My Medal:
Forevermore,
I place first.

A LETTER FROM FIRE

Dear Beautiful Fire,

Thank you for carrying your flame to the end.

You went on a beautiful journey from refinement to passionate. Let's take a moment to celebrate your eternal 1st place win because you walked through the fire and came out gold.

Trust and know that you can blaze within the flame, and the flame will blaze within you.

Remember *Fire* will

- Keep you warm even when darkness crouches at your door
- Never leave you nor forsake you
- Always refine you
- Tear down for you
- Dance high for you
- Shine for you and through you
- Honor you
- Cherish you
- Empower you and
- Eternally love you

Though the tangible gold is immaculate, know that your true victory starts from within and flows throughout.

Fierily, Beautiful Fire—

NOUSHKA

I AM BEAUTIFUL FIRE

HERE ARE 2 WAYS
TO KEEP THE FLAME GOING!

1. Download the 7 Ways to Live Your Life Ablaze

www.IAmBeautifulFire.com/7ways

This **free** guide will remind your fiery passions to flow from the inside out.

2. Flame on with Beautiful Fire on These Platforms

Tag #IAmBeautifuFire to showcase your experience with this collection.

YouTube: @IAmBeautifulFire
Instagram: @IAmBeautifulFire
TikTok: @IAmBeautifulFire
Pinterest: @IAmBeautifulFire
Twitter: @ImBeautifulFire
Facebook: I Am Beautiful Fire
Eventbrite: IAmBeautifulFire.eventbrite.com

ABOUT THE AUTHOR

From an eternal realm, Beautiful Fire, *NOUSHKA*, was destined to blaze forth as a writer/reciter, and her craft as one was written for her before the beginning of time.

As a child, she was often complimented for her beautiful handwriting, and though aesthetically pleasing, there were days of old when she naively inscribed her *aesthetic;* not realizing, everything written in this tangible realm has the ability to be trapped in time.

Now that she's met *Oneness*, whenever her pencil strikes paper, she writes from the *well* of, understanding, truth, and love.

To learn more about her and stay updated on the release of her next self-love collection, *When Fire Touched The Secret Place: A Poetic Exploration*, please visit:

www.IAmBeautifulFire.com

Made in United States
Orlando, FL
23 June 2023